Contents

Original text by Charles Applewhaite. Revised by Anne Pankhurst, Coach Education Director, The Lawn Tennis Association.

The publishers would like to thank Wilson for their photographic contribution to this book.

Photographs on front cover, back cover, inside back cover and pages 6, 7, 11 and 17 courtesy of Empics. Photograph on page 8 courtesy of Sporting Pictures. All other photographs courtesy of Allsport UK Ltd. Illustrations by Margaret Jones.

Note Throughout the book players and officials are referred to individually as 'he'. This should, of course, be taken to mean 'he or she' where appropriate. Similarly, the instructions in the text are geared towards right-handed players; left-handers should simply reverse these instructions.

Foreword

This book can be read by all age groups, from beginners coming to the game for the first time, to regular players and to those interested in the game, as parents or spectators. I recommend this book as an excellent introduction to our sport.

Sue Wolstenholme
Director
British Tennis Foundation

The court

The doubles court is larger than the singles court by an area as shown in fig. 1, popularly known as the 'tramlines'. The lines are marked in white, usually chalk, tape or paint.

The game as we know it today was developed from real (royal) tennis which had its origins in monastic times. Its first outdoor version was played in the gardens of stately homes in Britain in the 1870s, hence the name 'lawn tennis'. Its popularity grew quickly both in Britain and abroad and, partly because many countries lacked suitable lawns and others wished to play all the year round, other surfaces were introduced. These range from the fine clay courts of Europe to the cement courts of California.

In Britain the majority of courts are now low maintenance surfaces. They are constructed of asphalt, porous concrete and macadam, cushioned acrylic (or American cement) or artificial grass.

Loose surface hard courts are again becoming popular but they require regular attention, as does grass on which play is confined to the summer months. Indoor play world-wide is more and more popular. These indoor courts are mainly non-porous cushioned acrylic or carpet.

The surface used is critical to playing performance, particularly in top-class tennis. Asphalt, porous macadam and shale courts put a heavy brake on the bounce of the ball and allow it to be returned more easily. So these surfaces tend to encourage long rallies and defensive play. However, cement and similar smooth surfaces do not 'hold' the ball to the same extent and allow winners to be hit more easily. Grass is also fast, when it is hard and closely cut, thus encouraging the serve-and-volley tactics seen at Wimbledon.

In fig. 1 the length of the net is shown for doubles play. Nearly all courts have their net posts sited in this way. When singles matches are played, however, special singles sticks 3½ ft (1.07 m) high should be used to support the net from positions 3 ft (0.91 m) outside each singles sideline.

When adjusting the net it should first be raised by the net post winder until it is taut and then eased down to a height of 3 ft (0.91 m) with the centre band adjustment. The net should be slackened after play to reduce strain on the posts. Turn the bottom of the net over the net band to avoid fraying when the wind blows.

▼ *Fig. 1 Court dimensions*

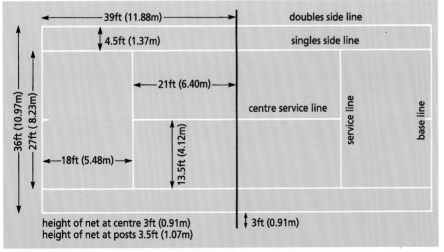

39ft (11.88m) — doubles side line

4.5ft (1.37m) — singles side line

21ft (6.40m)

36ft (10.97m)

27ft (8.23m)

centre service line

service line

base line

13.5ft (4.12m)

18ft (5.48m)

height of net at centre 3ft (0.91m)
height of net at posts 3.5ft (1.07m)

3ft (0.91m)

Equipment

Rackets

By far the most important item is the racket you use. Under the rules a racket must not exceed 32 in (81.28 cm) in length, or $12^{1/2}$ in (31.75 cm) in width, but it can be of any weight or shape.

The usual weight of senior length rackets is between 13 and 14 oz (325–350 g). Young players should start off with one of the specially made short-handled rackets. There are currently a variety of different lengths of racket to suit children from the age of 3 or 4 years upwards. The time of transition between various lengths will be determined by the height and ability of the child.

The balance of senior rackets is a matter of individual choice, as is the size of the grip. Evenly balanced rackets are to be recommended rather than those weighted in the head or the handle. Suitable grip sizes range from 4–$4^{1/2}$ in (10.1–11.5 cm). Choose a size and shape of grip that feels comfortable in your hand.

Rackets are now made of steel, aluminium, plastics, glassfibre, carbon and composites in place of the traditional wooden frame. Larger-headed and longer length rackets have also been introduced in recent years. These aim to increase the size of the 'sweet spot' – that area of the strings from which the ball can be returned without harshness.

Natural gut stringing is more resilient but more expensive and less durable than synthetic strings. The majority of rackets today are strung with synthetics and they have the advantage of being unaffected by wet weather, unlike gut. When it is not in use keep your racket in a cool, even temperature. Do not keep a racket in a waterproof cover for long periods.

Balls

It is advisable to use good quality balls. Balls that are badly worn with smooth covers are more difficult to control than new balls with plenty of nap. There are two types of ball – those that are inflated during manufacture and those that have no internal pressure. If you have to make the balls you buy last for several months then the latter type is better since they maintain a uniform bounce. *See* fig. 3 for the dimensions of a ball.

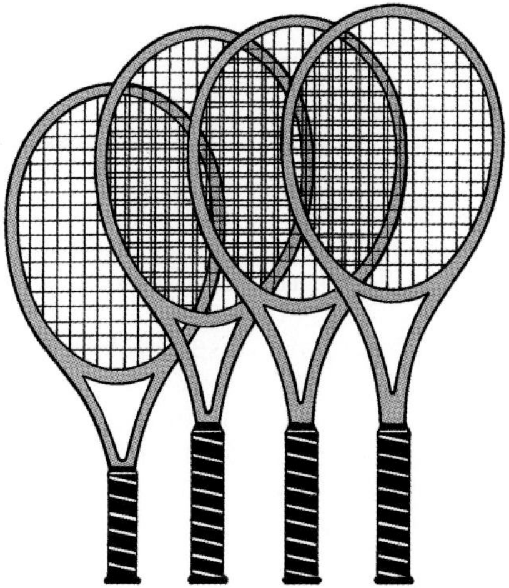

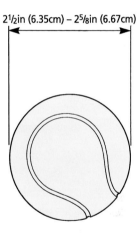

▲ *Fig. 3 Ball dimensions*

2½in (6.35cm) – 2⅝in (6.67cm)

▲ *Fig. 2 Racket lengths should increase as the young player grows older*

Clothing

Tennis is a fast and athletic game and the selection of comfortable clothing allowing unrestricted movement is very important. Clothing should be sweat-absorbent and although most tennis clothing now includes colour, the general rule, especially in tournament play, is for it to be predominantly white. Men usually wear shorts and short-sleeved shirts, and track suits for warmth before and after play. Women have a wide choice of dresses, and skirts or shorts with shirts or blouses. Special tennis socks which protect the feet while providing maximum comfort are available.

Headbands of various colours are sometimes worn to keep the hair under control and prevent it obscuring the vision during play.

In warm weather perspiration tends to run into the palm of the playing hand. To prevent this, absorbent and elasticated wrist-bands of towel-like material are worn by many tournament players.

Great attention should be given to the choice of tennis shoes. These should provide firm support for the feet, and shoes with a cushioned insole help to relieve tiredness. Do not choose shoes with smooth soles, except for when playing on special indoor surfaces. You need a good sole pattern to provide traction on the playing surface – rather like a car tyre. Players normally have different shoes for playing on different surfaces and in different conditions.

Singles

The game is started by one player serving. The question of who serves first and who has the choice of ends is decided by a toss. The winner of the toss may select one of four choices:

- elect to serve – in which case the opponent has choice of ends
- elect to receive – in which case the opponent has choice of ends
- choose ends – in which case the opponent may elect to serve or receive
- request the opponent to choose.

The first point of the game is started with the server standing behind the baseline between the imaginary extensions of the centre mark and the right-hand singles line. The receiver can take up any position he thinks most suitable on his side of the net.

A service stroke is completed when the racket touches the ball or the server attempts to strike it. A service is in play if it passes over the net without bouncing and falls within the service court diagonally opposite the server. The server has a second attempt to do this in each point if his first service is a fault. After each point has been scored the server changes to the other side of the centre mark for the next point, and so on.

On completion of the first game the player who was the receiver becomes the server in the next game. The players then serve in alternate games until the end of the match. The only exception to this is if the tie-break procedure is being used (*see* page 16).

Service

In delivering the service the server should:

- not serve until the receiver is ready. If the receiver is not ready a **let** is called, meaning that the service does not count and is to be taken again. If, however, the receiver attempts to play the ball he cannot then claim a let for not being ready
- place the ball into the air by hand
- strike the ball with his racket before it reaches the ground. If the server places the ball into the air but does not attempt a stroke then it is a **let**. If he attempts a stroke but misses the ball completely then it is a **fault**

- keep both feet to the correct side of the centre mark and not touch the baseline or court area with either foot until the ball has been hit. If not it is a **fault**
- not walk or run while delivering the service but slight movements of the feet are permitted.

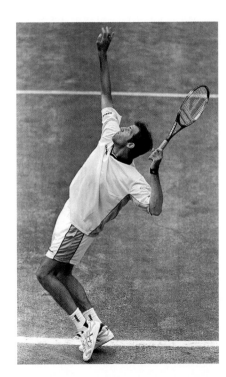

Order of service in a singles game

On completion of the first game, the player who has been the receiver becomes the server. The players then serve in alternate games until the end of the match. (But *see* (6) on page 16.)

Serving out of turn

If a player serves out of turn, the player who should have served must serve as soon as the mistake is discovered. All points scored up to this discovery will stand, but a single fault served before the discovery will not be counted. If the game is completed before the discovery is made, the order of the service remains as altered.

Faults

If the first service from the correct side is a fault, the server is allowed one more service from the same side.

If the first fault is due to a service from the wrong side the server may only deliver one more service from the correct side.

If the second service is a fault, making a 'double fault', the server loses the point. After a good service, play continues until a point is scored by either player.

A service ball striking the net, strap or band and bouncing directly into the correct service court is a **let** and that service must be played again.

A service ball striking any fixture other than the net is a **fault**.

Foot faults

The server may leave the ground while serving (fig. 4(a)) but it is a foot fault if, at the moment of striking the ball, the server touches the court or baseline with either foot (fig. 4(b)), or is on the wrong side of the baseline centre mark or beyond the imaginary extension of the sideline.

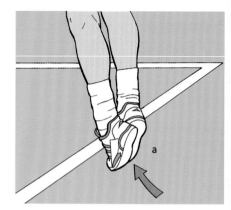

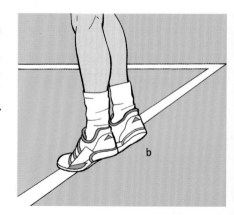

▶ *Fig. 4 Foot faulting*

Returning service

- A player returns the ball directly into his opponent's court before it bounces twice on his own side of the net. (**Good return.**)
- The ball touches the net, post, centre strap or net band, providing it passes over the net and falls within the opponent's court. (**Good return.**)
- The ball is returned outside the posts above or below the level of the top of the net and drops within the proper court. (**Good return.**)
- The server has served the ball. The receiver does not wait for the ball to bounce, but volleys it. (**Loses the point.**)
- The receiver deliberately carries or catches the ball on his racket or deliberately touches it with his racket more than once, i.e. a deliberate double hit. (**Loses the point.**)

- The ball bounces back over the net and the player on whose side it bounced reaches over the net and plays the ball. (**Good return** providing that neither he nor his racket touches the net, post or ground in his opponent's court.)
- He throws his racket and hits the ball. (**Loses the point.**)
- The ball touches the player or anything he wears or carries (except his racket) while the ball is in play. (**Loses the point.**)
- A player strikes the ball before it has crossed the net. (**Loses the point.**)
- A player succeeds in returning the ball which has struck another ball lying on the court. (**Good return.**)

Ball in and out

A ball is in play from the moment it is delivered in service (unless a fault or let is given) and remains in play until the point is decided.

Ball touching permanent fixture

If the ball in play (i.e. after the service) touches a permanent fixture (other than the net, posts, centre strap or net band) before it bounces, the striker loses the point. If it strikes the permanent fixture after it bounces, his opponent loses the point.

Ball in court

'A ball falling on a line is regarded as falling in the court bounded by that line' (Rule 22). Fig. 5 illustrates the correct interpretation of this rule. On a grass court the chalk is liable to fly

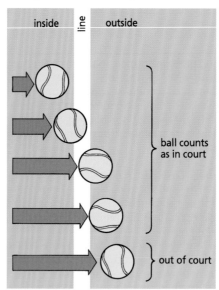

▼ *Fig. 5 Ball in and out of court*

inside | line | outside

ball counts as in court

out of court

even though the ball may bounce beyond the limits of the court, especially if the surface is worn or dusty. A puff of chalk should therefore not be regarded as conclusive evidence that the ball has touched the line.

Change of ends

The players change ends at the conclusion of the first, third and then every alternate game until the end of the set. If at the conclusion of the set the number of games played in that set is even, the players play one more game, i.e. the first game of the next set, before changing ends. When the number of games played in a set is uneven, the players change ends at the conclusion of that set and continue changing at the end of the first, third, fifth, seventh, etc. game until the set is finished.

Scoring

Game

The score of a player who has not won any points is said to stand at **Love**, and the first point any player (or pair in doubles) wins is called 15. The second point to the same player or pair is called 30, the third point is called 40 and the fourth point is called **Game**. The server's score is always given first. If A is serving to B and wins the first point the score is **Fifteen-Love** (i.e. 15 to A, and 0 to B). If B wins the first point the score is **Love-Fifteen** (i.e. 0 to A and 15 to B). When both players have won a point the score is **Fifteen-All** (i.e. 15 to A, and 15 to B), and so on.

Deuce

If the players score three points each (i.e. 40 to A, and 40 to B) the score is called **Deuce**. In this case A or B must win two consecutive points to win the game. If A wins the next point the score is **Advantage server** or **Advantage in**, A being the server. If B wins the point the score is **Advantage striker** or **Advantage out**. Should the score be Deuce and A wins the next point (**Advantage in**) but loses the following point, the score becomes **Deuce** again, and so on until either A or B leads by two points to win the game.

Set

The first player (or pair) to win six games wins the set, except that should the score become five games each – **Five-All** – one player or pair must go two games ahead to win the set (except when a tie-break procedure is operating; *see* page 16).

Match

The maximum number of sets in a match is five for men and three for women. Local tournament rules usually stipulate the number of sets to be played in a match, but normally matches are decided on the best of three sets.

Doubles

The court dimensions for doubles are shown in fig. 1. Service and choice of ends are decided by tossing as in the singles game (*see* page 8).

Order of service

The pair serving first must decide which partner will serve in the opening game. The opposing pair decides who will serve in the second game. Supposing A and B (fig. 6) win the toss and choose to serve. If A decides to serve in the opening game and C chooses to serve in the second game, B will serve in the third game and D in the fourth game. A serves again in the fifth game and service continues A, C, B, D, A, C, B, D, etc., until the set is ended. The order may be changed only at the beginning of a new set.

Ball touching server's partner

The service is a fault if the ball touches the server's partner or anything which he wears or carries.

Ball touching receiver's partner

If the service is otherwise good but the ball touches the receiver's partner or anything he wears or carries, either before or after bouncing in court, the server scores the point.

▼ *Fig. 6 Doubles*

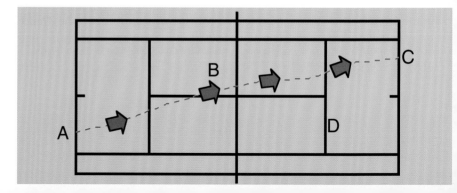

Serving out of turn

If a player serves out of turn the partner who ought to have served must serve as soon as the mistake is discovered, but any points scored and any fault served before the discovery will stand. If a game is completed before the mistake is discovered, the order of serving will remain as altered.

The server stands behind the baseline between an imaginary continuation of the centre mark and the doubles sideline (outer tram-line).

Order of receiving service

Partners must decide who is to receive in the right court and who in the left. Once the right court player (C in fig. 6) has stood to receive service, neither he nor his partner can change sides for receiving service until the start of a new set.

Error in order of receiving

If a player receives in the wrong court, he continues in that court until the end of the game but reverts to his correct court in the next receiving game of that set. There is no rule requiring the player who receives first in the first game to serve in the second game. Although C chooses to receive first, either of the pair may be the first to serve, but whoever commences serving must do so from the right side. Thus C can serve in either the second or fourth game. Once this order of service has been established it must be kept throughout the set, i.e. A, D, B, C, etc.

Tie-break procedure

The ITF has agreed that the following tie-break system may be used as an alternative to the scoring system laid down in the Rules of Tennis.

The tie-break will operate when the score reaches six games all in any set, except in the third or fifth set of a three-set or five-set match respectively, when an ordinary advantage set may be played in accordance with Rule 27.

The Organising Committee must decide and announce before the start of any tournament, match or competition whether the tie-break will operate at six games all or eight games all.

Where a decision is taken to operate the tie-break at eight games all, the Organising Committee may change this to six games all in one or more complete rounds of any event if, in their opinion, such action is in the best interests of the event.

Singles

(1) The player who first wins seven points shall win the game and the set provided he leads by a margin of two points. If the score reaches six points all, the game shall be extended until this margin has been achieved. Numerical scoring shall be used throughout the tie-break game.

(2) The player whose turn it is to serve shall be the server for the first point. His opponent shall be the server for the second and third points, and thereafter each player shall serve alternately for two consecutive points until the winner of the game and set has been decided.

(3) From the first point, each service shall be delivered alternately from the right and left courts, beginning from the right court.

(4) Players shall change ends after every six points and at the conclusion of the tie-break game.

(5) The tie-break game shall count as one game for the ball change.

(6) For the purpose of rotation of service the player (or pair) who served first in the tie-break game shall receive service in the first game of the following set.

Doubles

In doubles the same procedure as for singles shall apply. The player whose turn it is to serve shall be the server for the first point. Thereafter each player shall serve in rotation for two points, in the same order as previously in that set, until the winners of the game and set have been decided.

Match play

Accepting the umpire's decision

When there is an umpire, his decision is final on all questions of fact. An appeal to the referee (if there is one) can only be allowed on questions of law.

A linesman is responsible for line decisions but where there is an umpire then he, and not the players, is responsible for all line decisions. The umpire may overrule a linesman's decision if in his opinion a wrong call has been made. If either an umpire or a linesman gives an erroneous decision and then corrects himself the point must be replayed if the umpire considers that either player has been hindered.

Postponement of matches

The referee may postpone matches on account of darkness, the condition of the court or the weather. When a match is postponed the players will resume from the point of interruption unless the referee and the players unanimously agree otherwise.

Play shall be continuous

Play must be continuous from the first service until the match is concluded. Play can never be suspended, delayed or interrupted for the purpose of enabling a player to recover his strength or to receive advice. In tournament play, however, when players change ends, an interval of not more than 90 seconds is allowed from the time the last ball was played to the start of the next game.

At the end of each set the players are allowed a 2-minute rest. At the first changeover of the next set the players do not have a rest.

Basic tactics

Put and keep the ball in play

It should be obvious but many players do seem to forget this principle: try to hit the ball to a consistent length. If you can keep your opponent behind the baseline, he will find it more difficult to hit a winning shot.

It is not necessary to hit 'winners' to win matches. Most matches are lost by a player making too many mistakes. If a player *always* returns the ball into play, he will force his opponent into losing the match. The good player develops a balance between consistency and aggression, combining soft shots with hard ones. As players improve, this balance becomes even more important.

Retain a good position on court

The better your position on court in relation to the play, the easier it is to execute the stroke. The basic positions for singles and doubles are shown on the following pages.

Many players appreciate the need to move quickly to retrieve an opponent's shot, but fail to use the same quick movements to recover to a good, ready position in relation to the play.

Make your opponent run

It is important that an opponent has little time in which to play his shots and that he has regularly to change position to play his shots. It is well known how easy it is to 'groove' a shot by hitting it from the same position regularly. If you don't want your opponent to get into a rhythmic groove, move him around the court (i.e. from left to right, with high and low shots, and with short and long length).

Exploit a weakness

From the opening practice shots in a match, a player should be assessing his opponent's play and searching for any weaknesses. However, don't overdo this tactic, otherwise you will lose an element of surprise. Be prepared to vary the pace of your shots.

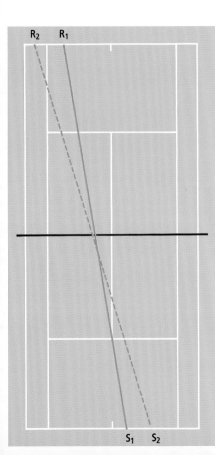

Singles

Basic positions on court

◀ *Fig. 7 Service and return – **S1**: the server is positioned behind the baseline near the centre mark. **R1**: the receiver is positioned just on or outside the baseline, covering both sides of the service area equally. **S2**: the server may adjust his position to create greater angles against the receiver. **R2**: the receiver may adjust his position to counter any change of position by the server*

▶ *Fig. 8 Rallying in play – **S1**: the server is now positioned up to 3–5 ft (1–1¹/₂ m) behind the baseline near the centre mark. **R1**: the receiver is now positioned up to 3–5 ft (1–1¹/₂ m) behind the baseline. The players will adjust their positions to take account of varying angles and depth of shots. They may decide to move to the positions **S2** and **R2**, 7–10 ft (2–3 m) from the net. Players at the net will also adjust their positions to take account of varying angles, and the depth and height of shots. The positions on court are never fixed: they must reflect the pattern of play*

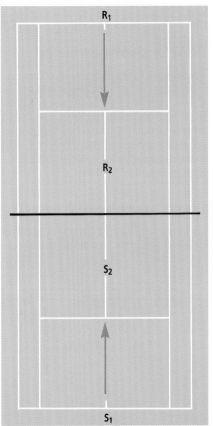

Doubles

Basic positions on court

Many players feel more relaxed in doubles than in singles, and enjoy the shared responsibility. However, doubles still requires good tactics and strategy and, as part of a team, you must be aware of the strengths and weaknesses of your partner and your opposition.

Playing positions

Players will change their positions to develop possible winning positions. Remember:

- retain good positions on court
- doubles is a team game, so all tactics must take this into consideration
- attack the weaker opponent
- win your service game
- play as a team.

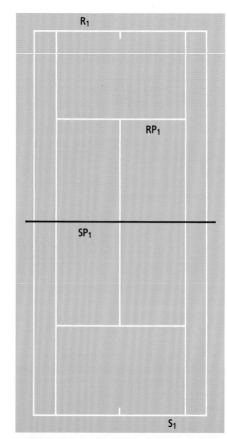

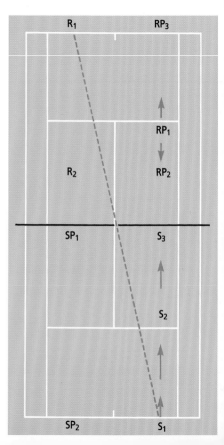

Fig. 9 (far left) Serve and return – S1: the server is positioned behind the baseline, a little wider of the centre mark than for singles. SP1: the server's partner is positioned close to the net, approximately half-way between the outside line and the centre service line. R1: the receiver adopts the same position as in singles. RP1: the receiver's partner stands just outside the left-hand service area, an equal distance between the inner sideline and the centre service line

Fig. 10 (left) (a) The server may move from the baseline through midcourt (S2) to a volley position (S3), developing a joint attacking position with his partner, SP1. (b) The receiver's position and that of his partner will be controlled by the standard of the return of service. (c) Receiver R1 will hold his position after the return of service. His partner, RP1, should move slightly forwards to RP2. Alternatively, RP1 may choose to go back to the baseline (RP3) to develop a joint defensive position with his partner, R1. (d) The receiver may follow the return to the net (R2). He joins his partner, RP2, to develop a balanced attacking position. (e) If lobbed, the server's partner, SP1, may go back to SP2, again to develop a joint defensive position with his partner, S1.

Spin

Many players apply spin to the ball. Some grips, such as the semi-Western on the forehand and the chopper on the service (*see* pages 29 and 31), actually facilitate the application of spin.

Why is spin used?

There are three major reasons why spin, usually either topspin or slice, is used:

- because the strategies and tactics of tennis demand it
- because it can confuse an opponent and upset his playing rhythm
- because equipment and different court surfaces ensure its effectiveness.

What does spin do?

The application of spin affects the following:

- the rotation of the ball through the air
- the ball's flight path through the air
- the bounce of the ball
- the flight of the ball after the bounce.

Applying spin

To impart topspin on a groundstroke the racket head should start below and finish above the contact point on the ball, making a sharp upward swing.

To slice a groundstroke the racket head should start above and finish below the contact point of the ball, making a downward swing.

Effects of spin

The path and angle of the ball's flight before the bounce determines its path and angle after the bounce.

The principles of spin apply when serving. For example, a sliced serve bounces considerably lower than does a topspin serve. There may also be a degree of swing in the ball's flight path.

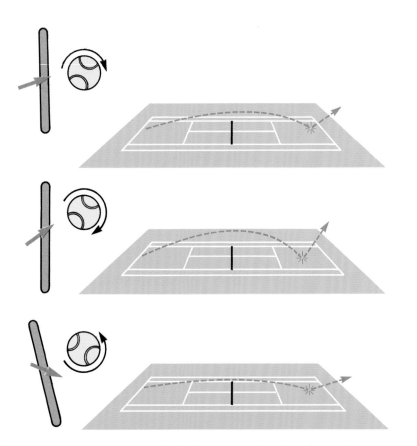

Developing tactics

As you get better at playing tennis and at executing the strokes, you will need to develop your tactical knowledge if you are to improve further the quality of your game. Don't forget the basic matchplay tactics which should be the 'building blocks' of your game.

◀ Fig. 11 (top) Lifted groundstroke: slight forward rotation of the ball. The ball bounces in a regular manner

◀ Fig. 12 (middle) Topspin groundstroke: forward rotation of the ball. Increased air pressure above the ball forces it to dip at the end of its flight. The bounce is generally higher than on a lifted groundstroke

◀ Fig. 13 (bottom) Slice groundstroke: backward rotation of the ball. Increased air pressure below the ball lifts it and keeps it in the air longer. The bounce is generally lower than on a lifted groundstroke

Court area

The court area is an important tactical aspect in terms of its space, i.e. the height, width and depth into which the ball can be played. As your awareness of the court area improves, and your techniques develop, so you will be able to place the ball tactically and so make your opponent run around in order to reach it. For tactical reasons the court area can be sub-divided as follows. (*See* fig. 14.)

Attack and defence

Playing in specific areas of the court makes certain shots more (or less) possible. The following are influencing factors when you make contact with the ball:

● your position on court
● your opponent's position on court
● the height of the ball when contact is made.

The **defence zone** is the baseline area and the area from which it is difficult to hit winning shots. You must:

● rally consistently from different positions on the baseline
● counter-attack by taking the ball early
● move quickly in order to play the ball on your strongest side.

The **manoeuvring zone** is the mid-court area from which it is possible to pressurise an opponent and begin to build a winning situation. You must:

● move from defence through to attack with a good approach shot to set up a strong net position
● select the right shot, forcing or winning
● move quickly to play the ball at its optimum height (which is often dictated by the court surface).

The **attack zone** is the net area from which it should be possible to make winning shots. You must:

● play attacking volleys from above the height of the net
● play defensive volleys on fast balls or on those which are below the height of the net

● move quickly in any direction in order to play effective volleys and smashes.

When you fully appreciate the principles of the court zones, you should then be able to develop your knowledge and use it to work out varying strategies for successful play in the different zones.

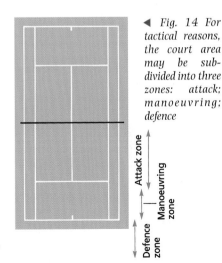

◀ *Fig. 14 For tactical reasons, the court area may be sub-divided into three zones: attack; manoeuvring; defence*

Warm-up

In your enthusiasm to start playing tennis don't be tempted to forego the warm-up, even if it is only a simple one. Warming up has several benefits: it physically prepares the body for exercise, which means that the risks of injury to muscles, ligaments and tendons are greatly reduced, and also that the heart is accustomed to increased activity; and it helps a player to begin concentrating on the match or practice before him.

Start by gentle jogging up and down on the spot, or from side to side, or forwards and backwards. You will also find that jogging a short distance around the court is helpful.

Then move on to stretch each part of the body – neck, arms, trunk and legs – separately. Here are a few exercise suggestions (remember to wear something warm when you are doing your exercises).

Neck

Bend your head from side to side, backwards and forwards and from shoulder to shoulder. Do *not* attempt a full circular movement, since this is harmful to the vertebra at the top of the neck.

Arms

Circle both arms together forwards and backwards in a large movement. Small circles can be performed when each arm is extended out to the side and is level with the shoulder. Another exercise involves crossing your arms in front of your chest and then swinging each outwards and upwards to the side. The arms may also be swung behind you so that the backs of your hands meet roughly half-way down your back. (But don't be too vigorous in your movement: the aim is to stretch and warm up in a controlled manner.)

Trunk

With your hands on your hips, move your hips in a large circle, first one way and then the other. Keeping your back straight, bend over to the right and to the left. The stretch may be increased on about the third attempt by bending the outside arm over your head.

Trunk circling is another helpful exercise: raise your arms above your head and then move them together to one side, down in front of your body and on up to the other side. Repeat, but going in the opposite direction: it is always important to work both sides of the body and not to concentrate on just one side.

Legs

Widen your stance so that your feet are well spread and bend forwards from the waist, always making sure your back is 'flat'. Reach forwards, between your splayed legs and behind you. A variation is to fold your arms in front of you when bending forwards and to hold the stretch position for a minimum of five seconds. Do *not* 'bounce' your back in an attempt to reach further down, as this puts undue pressure on the lower back and can result in injury.

Stretch hamstrings by crossing your legs over so that the outsides of your feet touch each other. Then slowly try to place your palms on the ground in front of you. Don't worry if you can't reach the floor: the main emphasis should be on gentle stretching of each hamstring.

Further stretching of leg muscles involves lowering your body weight over one knee while keeping the other straight. Hold the stretch for five seconds before changing the stance and following the same procedure for the other leg.

These exercises form just a brief selection from the many that are recommended by coaches. Find out as much as you can about them, but don't try to do too much too soon. By regularly following the routine of neck, arms, trunk and legs you will be well on your way to developing a good self-protection system.

Note Remember that all these exercises should be slow, steady stretches.

The mental game

Reasons for playing

Do you play tennis to meet people and socialise, to get physical exercise, to win competitions, or purely for enjoyment, or for a combination of these? Whatever the reason, try to retain your own basic philosophy for playing and gradually introduce other areas to add to your pleasure of the game.

The better players are not always those with the best technique or physique. Innumerable matches are won by players who are able to use their brains to find a way of winning when the obvious advantages appear to be totally in the opponent's favour.

What do you need to be successful in developing the right mental attitude? Here are some pointers.

Analysis

Your method of play

Are you steady and consistent, or aggressive and happy to take risks? Whichever is your method, try to recognise your strengths and weaknesses, and then plan your matchplay around them. Remember that the way you play tennis is usually just an extension of your personality and how you take on life.

Opponent's method of play

Can you 'read' your opponent's method and style of play – have you noticed a technique that cracks under pressure or a movement pattern that leaves gaps on his side of the court?

Tennis can be described as being similar to a game of chess, except of course that players are continually active and there is only around three seconds between moves. So, your decision-making processes need to be well practised and rapidly implemented.

Assessing your performance

In competition it is very easy to think 'I won; I played well' or 'I lost; I played badly'. You should differentiate between the result and your level of performance. In winning or losing, did you perform as well as usual? That should be your measure for personal success.

Developing the four 'Cs'

Challenge

Every time you step on to a tennis court you will meet new challenges, some from your opponent and some from within yourself. Look upon these as positive challenges and enjoy the contest. You can discover many truths about yourself in the testing conditions of a tennis match.

Concentration

Whether you are analysing an opponent's technique, matchplay strategy or even watching for spin on the ball, you need a certain level of concentration or 'focus'. Try to be methodical in your focusing on a specific aspect. If you flit from one object to another, you will find it very difficult to achieve effective concentration. For example, a positive aid to concentrating on the flight of the ball is to say quietly 'bounce' exactly as the ball bounces and 'hit' as you make contact.

Confidence

Confidence comes from self-belief in your ability to reach a level of performance that you have set as your current goal. However, try not to set goals that are too high and that you are always missing. Conversely, don't set easy goals that you can reach without a challenge.

Effective goal-setting through the use of realistic short- and medium-term goals can be the basis from which to develop a high level of self-confidence.

Competition

Competition comes from the love of a challenge. A true competitor is one who 'hangs in' all the way, whether he is in front or behind in the match. In every tennis match there is always one winner and one loser, but there should always be two competitors. If you have tried to give of your best all the way, there can be no disgrace in defeat. Being a competitor can help you learn many positive aspects about yourself.

Sportsmanship

Sport provides a wonderful opportunity to meet and compete with others. However, as well as written rules and regulations, there are also unwritten codes of behaviour.

When playing and competing make sure you behave as you would wish others to behave towards you. In other words:

- try to appreciate not only your own good play but also your opponent's
- be fair and honest about all decisions and calls
- don't allow any compelling desire to win to compromise your sportsmanship and behaviour. Sport should be fun!

Practice

Practice is the major factor in tennis improvement. It is a good idea to plan it into small, manageable periods of time.

To get the most out of your practice time you should work on specific points of strokeplay, shots or targets. Begin with simple controlled skills and then develop the practice through the use of pace, width, movement, etc. If you run into difficulties, backtrack to a simpler level, regain your confidence and then try to raise the level again.

Disciplined thinking helps players to practise intelligently. So, plan your sessions around the reality of match play. Choosing partners is also important: tennis is generally considered to be a game for 'individuals', but in order to improve it is helpful for two individuals to form a 'team' and to benefit from co-operation in practice. Anyone who is willing to hit, or even throw, tennis balls in a controlled manner will be of value in practice sessions. For example, parents can help their children by using simple feeding methods. Taking a basket of balls, they can feed single ones in succession to simulate a ball machine.

Wall practices

Tennis skills can be improved and practised successfully without tennis courts, as long as players use their imagination and all the facilities that are available to them. They will soon begin to realise that although it is preferable to be on a court, it is still possible to have an enjoyable practice when no court is available.

Practising against a wall is one of the finest ways of developing basic skills. Walls are generally easily accessible and players do not have to rely on anyone else for a partner. They can practise at their own level of control and speed without feeling under pressure to give another player correct feeding and ball placement.

Practising against a wall should not be allowed to fall into a casual, unmotivated 'slap around', because this can well 'groove' the poor shots that the player is trying to eradicate. You should aim to construct practices and exercises that fire your enthusiasm to reach a target, a level of technical competence.

Techniques

Grips

When learning how to play tennis it is advisable to adopt one of the following most effective grips for specific shots. When you are more experienced you can then decide whether or not to modify your grips. The most important factor is to be able to control the racket at all times, but especially on contact with the ball. A grip, therefore, needs to be strong but flexible and, most importantly, comfortable.

Semi-Western forehand

This grip is used primarily for the forehand drive. Whereas with the Eastern forehand grip the palm is placed behind the handle, here the palm lies underneath the handle.

This grip makes it easier to hit balls that are above waist height, and leads to aggressive forehands. It requires an open stance positioning for successful impact and control. The contact point is closer to the body than with the Eastern forehand grip (*see* page 30).

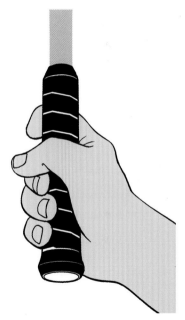

▲ *Fig. 15 Semi-Western forehand grip*

Eastern forehand

This is known as the Eastern or 'shake hands' grip, the latter because the palm is placed behind the handle and the thumb is wrapped round the grip as though 'shaking hands' with the racket. The index finger is slightly spread apart from the middle finger.

As well as being suitable for the forehand drive (*see* page 32), enabling a player to hit balls of varying height with maximum strength, it can also be used for the forehand volley and lob (*see* pages 39 and 43), and, most importantly, by novices for learning to serve (*see* page 38).

Eastern backhand

This is used for the backhand drive, the lob, and the early stages of the volley. To find the correct position, place the palm of your hand on top of the handle and then move the racket inwards by 90°. The thumb is positioned diagonally across the back of the handle, although some players just wrap their thumb around the back. This is a very sensitive, as well as a strong, grip.

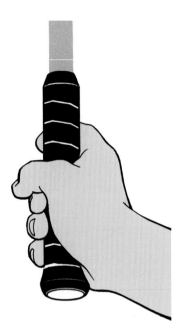

▲ *Fig. 16 Eastern forehand or 'shake hands' grip*

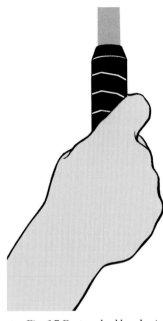

▲ *Fig. 17 Eastern backhand grip*

Two-handed backhand

The two-handed backhand provides greater strength and flexibility than a one-handed grip. The hand nearest the end of the racket should be holding the racket with a Continental grip (*see* fig. 19). The added hand could be in an Eastern forehand grip. Both hands should be close together and touching each other on the handle.

Young players just starting may often choose to hold the racket with two Eastern forehand grips. This does not involve a grip change, the free hand merely being added to support the other. It is a helpful grip for youngsters, but is not the most suitable for more advanced adult play.

Chopper/Continental

The chopper grip is used mainly for the service and for advanced stages of the volley. It is half-way between the Eastern forehand and backhand, and involves placing the palm of the hand on top of the racket for the service. It provides greater racket head speed, flexibility and variation than does the straightforward forehand grip.

Young players new to tennis may prefer to serve with their forehand grips. This should be discouraged – the right grip will develop their confidence, ability and enjoyment of the game.

▶ *Fig. 18 (right) Two-handed backhand grip*

▶ *Fig. 19 (far right) Chopper/Continental grip*

Basic strokes

Forehand drive

Semi-Western grip
This grip is commonly used in today's game. It is suitable for playing on courts with surfaces producing high-bouncing balls that can be hit above waist height. However, it has some disadvantages on very low balls, i.e. at ankle height.

This grip is very effective for using topspin on the basic shot.

The execution of the forehand drive using the semi-Western grip has many similarities to that using the Eastern grip, i.e. early preparation, sound foot-work and a controlled swing.

Start from the ready position (*see* page 46). Keeping your wrist firm and the racket head up, take the racket back early. Move smoothly into the forward swing, ensuring you have a semi-open stance with a completed backswing lower than the contact point of the ball.

Swing from a low to a high position and, maintaining a firm grip through-out, make contact with the ball at a point which is level with your front foot and a comfortable arm's length away from your body (the arm is slightly bent). Try to give a semi-brushing action up the ball to impart a little topspin.

Complete the stroke with a high follow-through and then go back to the ready position.

Eastern/'shake hands' grip
Start from the ready position (*see* page 46), with your knees slightly bent and your racket held in a relaxed manner in front of you. Take your racket back early and begin to turn your hips and shoulders so that you can play the ball from the side.

At this stage your body weight should be on your back foot. As your racket reaches the top of its back-swing, your body weight should begin to move forwards. Make sure the back swing flows smoothly via a loop into the forward swing, and then move for-wards positively into the shot.

Swing from a low to a high position, imagining your racket is an extension of your arm. You should actually hit the ball at a comfortable distance slightly in front of your leading hip, with the wrist kept firm on contact.

You'll achieve good balance if you let your shoulders and hips turn into the stroke, transferring your weight on to your front foot. The stroke is fin-ished with a high follow-through in the direction you want the ball to go.

Go back to the ready position as soon as you have completed the shot.

Backhand drive

Eastern grip

Adopt the ready position (*see* page 46). Take the racket back early and, using the left hand to support the racket, change your grip. The left hand continues to support the racket throughout the backswing. You should turn your shoulders and hips to the left to enable you to execute the stroke from a side-on position.

As the racket reaches the end of the backswing, drop smoothly into the forward swing with a shallow loop. As with the forehand drive, you should be aiming to hit from a low to a high position.

Transfer your weight on to your leading foot as you step into the shot and make contact with the ball a comfortable distance from, and slightly in front of, the leading foot.

Make sure you watch the ball on to the strings and that you keep a firm grip on the racket, especially as the ball is hit. Follow through in front of your body in the direction you want the ball to go, all the time maintaining your balance.

After the stroke has been completed, go back to the ready position, facing the net.

▼ *Fig. 22 Backhand drive (Eastern grip)*

Two-handed backhand

The advantage of this shot is that it can be used by players who are not physically strong enough to hold the racket with one hand on the backhand side: the added hand enables the player to control the racket face and swing, and it also means the ball can be hit with power.

The disadvantage is that it may limit a player's reach. So, it is vital to get into a good position if you want to play this stroke. However, in competition this may not always be possible.

The two-handed backhand has the same preparation and swing as the one-handed backhand. The ball is hit at a comfortable arm's length away from the body, just about level with the leading hip. The contact point tends to be slightly closer than with the single-handed stroke. For the follow-through, which is high and in front of the body, the arms should be well out from the body.

▶ *Fig. 23 Backhand drive (two-handed grip)*

The service

Beginners may prefer to practise the serve using the Eastern forehand grip. To become more proficient, however, they must adopt the chopper, or Continental, grip. The chopper grip is the most effective grip for developing a variety of services.

The ready position is a comfortable sideways position, with your feet shoulder-width apart. Your front foot should be pointing slightly towards the opposite net post and your back foot should be parallel with the baseline.

Begin with the racket and ball held together (it's easier to cope with one ball rather than two at first), roughly pointing in the direction in which you are aiming, Relax!

Maintaining good balance throughout, throw the ball (technically known as 'placing the ball') from your fingertips into the air at a comfortable height and slightly towards your target. With practice, you will be able to work both hands together in a rhythmical fashion. It is a good idea to place the ball just above your full reach (with the racket) so that you hit it just as it begins to fall – when it is almost stationary in the air. Make sure your place-up arm does not go too much to one side, but to the front, and that you release the ball when your arm is straight.

Bend your knees and arch your back slightly for power and control when you throw the racket head at the ball. You should make contact with the ball at your maximum reach with a firm, but flexible, grip. Follow through in the direction of the ball to complete the stroke at the left side of the body. Then recover to the ready position.

Many players leave the ground as they reach up to hit the ball. They then land on the front foot. In fig. 24 the player lands on the back foot. Either is acceptable but more players now land on their front foot after the serve.

Forehand volley

From the technical point of view, the volley is the simplest of all the strokes. However, because the ball is played before it bounces, and because you are now nearer to your opponent, you must be able to react quickly in order to execute it properly.

Beginners will probably try to adopt the Eastern forehand grip at first, but, with low volleys possibly causing problems they are advised to move on to the chopper, or Continental, grip. This can be used for either the forehand or the backhand volley, which is particularly useful on those occasions when there is insufficient time in which to change the grip.

Practise volleying from a position about 6–10 ft (2–3 m) in front of the net. Watch the ball right on to the racket strings, and try to preserve good balance at all times.

Starting from the ready position, with your knees slightly bent and your racket supported by your free hand, prepare early with a short backswing – the racket should go no further than the shoulder. Transfer your weight on to your forward foot as you hit the ball with a strong punching or blocking action when it is roughly level with this foot. Your hitting arm should be slightly bent and you should aim to make contact with the ball in front, and a little to the side, of your body. (Turning your shoulders well in advance, in other words as soon as you see the ball coming towards you, will help you put your racket in a good position.)

You must maintain a firm grip and wrist throughout the stroke, but especially when the racket meets the ball. There should be little, if any, follow-through so that you can recover quickly in case your shot is returned and you need to volley again.

▼ *Fig. 25 Forehand volley*

Backhand volley

A similar action to that employed for the forehand volley is used for the one-handed backhand volley, but this time the supporting hand stays on the racket until just before the ball is struck.

For the two-handed backhand volley the hands are placed next to each other on the grip. This restricts the player's reach, but often brings greater power to the shot than with the one-handed grip.

The key points to remember are:

• use a short backswing
• make contact with the ball with a slightly bent arm, a comfortable distance away from the body (turn your shoulders if you've got time)
• transfer your weight on to your leading foot as you step into the shot
• use a blocking or punching action to strike the ball
• use minimal follow-through, if at all
• always recover to the ready position so you are prepared for your opponent's return.

▼ *Fig. 26 Backhand volley*

Smash

If executed well, the smash can be an impressive winning shot. On the other hand, a player lacking in confidence can soon run into trouble if his opponent puts up a lob (*see* page 43) and he is unable to deal with it securely.

Similar in action to the service, the smash requires above all fast, balanced footwork to get you back up the court and beneath the ball. Then, ideally, you should be able to move forwards into the shot. The chopper grip is essential for smashing.

Start from the ready position, and run back in a sideways movement: this is easier than trying to run backwards. Once underneath the ball, you should also be in a sideways position so you avoid smashing directly into the net. As the racket is taken back to behind your shoulder in a shorter movement than that used for the service, it may help to point your free hand at the ball. This acts as a guide to the ball's flight path and also aids balance.

Then throw your racket head at the ball, keeping a firm but flexible grip, and strike the ball at your maximum reach. Since the ball is falling from a greater height than in the service, timing, accuracy and concentrated watching of its descent are critical here. Follow through in the direction of the ball and quickly recover to the ready position.

As you become more proficient at the smash, you can practise jumping to reach the ball. Good co-ordination is involved in synchronising the takeback and hitting of the ball with the leg movements.

Forehand lob

The lob can be a useful weapon in a player's armoury, because it can successfully interrupt the flow of groundstroke play. For the opponent accustomed to hard hitting or to being close to the net this may mean an unwelcome break in concentration or being forced into less proficient play.

The aim of the lob is to force your opponent back from the net by hitting the ball over his head, preferably over his backhand side, thereby making it hard for him to play a strong smash or even a good return.

From the ready position, take the racket back early and follow smoothly into the forward swing. As you step into the shot, transfer your weight on to your leading foot and swing from a very low to a very high position to give lift to the ball.

Playing the lob is similar to executing a forehand stroke, but the racket face is kept 'open' when it makes contact with the ball and the follow-through is a little higher than the forehand.

Keeping your grip firm but flexible, practise striking the ball when it is a comfortable arm's length away from the body and roughly level with your front hip. You will soon discover the effects different angles of the racket have on the ball's flight path. Imagine keeping the ball on the racket for as long as possible, as this helps to take some of the pace off it. Unless you add topspin, avoid hitting the ball too hard, otherwise your offensive tactic will be lost by the ball landing outside your opponent's baseline.

After completing the shot, recover to the ready position and be prepared for defensive measures if your lob was a poor one, or for a solid follow-up counter-attack if it was a good one.

▼ *Fig. 28 Forehand lob*

Backhand lob

The backhand lob mirrors the backhand drive, except that the racket face is kept open on impact with the ball, and the follow-through is slightly higher. Make sure you take the racket back early, change the grip accordingly and support the racket with your free hand until just before impact. Once again, step into the shot, transferring your weight to your leading foot, and swing from a very low to a very high position. After the follow-through go back to the ready position.

As an interesting exercise you might like to intersperse forehand and backhand drives with the lob occasionally. This will show you how strongly related the two strokes are, but also how much additional control is required for the lob.

▼ *Fig. 29 Backhand lob*

Ready position

Whether playing groundstrokes, or serving, or volleying, you must begin from what is called the ready position. Such a position enables you to start quickly, to get to the right place at the right moment for hitting the ball.

Groundstrokes

In preparing for a groundstroke, support the racket with your free hand: this is the best way to set yourself. (*See* fig. 30.) Use a relaxed forehand grip in the hitting hand, supporting the racket head in the free hand at the throat. (Two-handed players may hold the racket with both hands lightly touching each other.)

Your feet should be shoulder-width apart, your body should be bent over towards the racket head, and the knees should be slightly bent and springy. Your weight should be on the balls of your feet, not on your heels. Focus your eyes on the opponent.

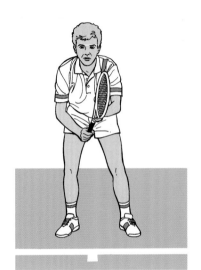

▲ *Fig. 30 Ready position (groundstroke)*

Service

For the service, the ready position is a comfortable sideways stance that provides a strong base for throwing. (*See* fig. 31.) Both feet must, of course, be behind the baseline, and they must be approximately shoulder-width apart. The hands should point towards the target, and the ball and racket should be together at the beginning of the swing.

▶ *Fig. 31 Ready position (service)*

Volleying/smashing

Again, this is an alert, springy position, with the racket supported at the throat by the free hand. The racket should be held above the height of the net, the feet are shoulder-width apart, the body is bent over towards the target, and the knees are bent slightly. (*See* fig. 32.) Your eyes should be focused on the opponent, and the overall impression is a more aggressive one since you are now nearer to your opponent.

Administration

The International Tennis Federation (ITF), which is made up of member countries' national associations, is responsible for the game's rules. These are carefully adhered to throughout the world.

For more information on the game and how to join a club, write to The Lawn Tennis Club Services Department, The Queen's Club, West Kensington, London W14 9EG.

◀ *Fig. 32 Ready position (volley/smash)*

Index